ABOUT THE AUTHOR

Working through many a mental health journey, concerned about sanity, anger and dignity, the understanding of not just life but different mental states that govern life would shape my future and designate my present and quantify my past. A fortunate airman in a new life with still the same troubles and problems but now with only a fictional poet as support, Gary embraces mental health and constantly questions sanity whilst exploring his mind and the world around him, finding solace in poetry where once again the words of life will take him through dark and meaningful times where no other support was available.

Gary Niel Hitching

RUN THEY SAID...
WAR OF THE MIND

Book 2 in the 'Run They Said'
poetry series

AUSTIN MACAULEY PUBLISHERS™
LONDON • CAMBRIDGE • NEW YORK • SHARJAH

A CIP catalogue record for this title is available from the
British Library.

ISBN 9781398490857 (Paperback)
ISBN 9781398490864 (ePub e-book)

www.austinmacauley.com

First Published 2022
Austin Macauley Publishers Ltd
1 Canada Square
Canary Wharf
London
E14 5AA

DEDICATION

To my dad who enjoyed my first book but couldn't read the rest. His raised eyebrows and tuts will be with me always, as will his support, love and tolerance.

POEMS

Noise

The noise continues in my head,
I thrash around in my bed ,
There is anger and fire everywhere,
And life goes on without a care.
I look at people with a different eye,
I walk the road and check the sky.
The moments of my past will never leave,
It's now for my mind to perceive
When violence comes like a tsunami wave
And my head is as high as a cave.
I sit and hide with no other,
No support from my band of brothers,
The mask of life I wear for all to see
Nobody will know the real me.

Upon leaving the military, the sights I saw in the various war zones still haunted me. Within the pages that follow are my recollections of these moments and vivid war memories, Leaving the military was the darkest period of my life: no support – just words on a page.

What You See

I am happy, never sad,
Placid, never mad.
The face will give nothing away
How deep and distant has been my day.
You walk up to me talk a while,
I hide all emotion behind a smile.
You laugh, you touch, you go about your day,
I wanted some help but just couldn't say.
When life turns you into a busy lonely man,
Nobody can tell or understand.
What they see is success and joy,
What I am is a lonely young boy
Stood on a plinth with nobody around
Covered in noise and making no sound.
So what you see is not quite right
And that's just the way I continue my plight.

Surrounding yourself with people can push you further into loneliness, as I soon found out through my new chosen career in the pub – probably not the best decision I ever made, but contending with the stress focused my mind onto other areas. A smile always reassured that everything was going well, when the reality of it was my mind submerging into further darker depths.

Say What You Mean

I think you misunderstood my actions,
You didn't weigh up the factions,
You judged before you knew.
You were filled with dread,
And got into my head,
I didn't mean to do what I do.
It's my mental ability
To test this facility,
My mind doesn't seem to play.
You're upset right now,
I really don't know how
Things turned out this way.
I have trouble working it out,
Which leads me to shout,
Saying things I shouldn't have said.
I should have thought things through,
Talked to you too,
But I listened to my head instead.
My Mental state
Is what I hate,
I have no clue of who I am or will be.
I will get through
I need help too,
Dealing with life and PTSD.

I realised very quickly I was ill and had nowhere to turn. This made me further turn to poetry and refer to the poet as my helper, a dangerous road to lead but the safer option rather than telling people I had mental health problems and constantly thought dark demons and thoughts. The overwhelming voice of the past, "Nobody likes a sissy," was constantly with me.

Progress

You died last week and I didn't notice.
That is what people call progress.
You succeeded last month and we didn't care.
When you mention it people just stare.
I killed someone last year,
It happens so much, there will be no fear.
I saved someone's life not long ago,
No thanks for it, now nothing to show.
Everybody seems to just think about themselves,
No concerns about real mental health,
But to start the healing process
Surely we should think about progress.
Progress can be as little as a thank you,
A morning wave asking, "How do you do?"
A knock on the door to check on someone,
To listen without prejudice, opinion none.
Progress is shown in a number of ways
To allow a change in the monotony of days.
When you change the day with the happiness of light,
Progress will happen over night.
Next time somebody does something they should,
Say, "Thank you," and acknowledge progress is good.

With no guidance on how to act and what to do anymore as the protective cloak of the military had been snatched, I chose a number of mantras to try and be a better person and push the dark thoughts away by immersing deep within the community. Sadly, you can only immerse as deep as people want and will allow you to, as I soon found out.

Pause for Thought

Pause for thought,
That what I was taught.
When you don't know which way to turn,
Pause for thought.
Allow dreams to be caught,
And lots of respect will be earned.
Pause for thought,
Decisions are sought,
The goal will be achieved not yearned.
Pause for thought,
Unconscious actions are thwart,
Consequences are left unturned.
A moment away from stress,
Making sense of your mess,
Try it and you will see
That pausing for thought some time
Makes time seem sublime
And gives moments away from insanity.

Continuing on my mantra pathway, paving out my new rules for the changed person I was to become, expelling the person of the past was my way forward, but unfortunately when you forget or hide your past, it has a habit of reminding you.

PTSD and ME

When a person has seen suffering and pain
There life can never be the same.
The rage and fear that burns inside
Sweeps in like a rampant spring tide.
No control of the rage that follows
Or the guilt and remorse in which the victim wallows.
A legacy or karma some might say
Of the sight of horrific war-torn days
To win a war and liberate through destruction and force
With little or none and hidden remorse.
The revenge for this forever will stay with me
Like an angry snake in the form of PTSD,
Sitting inside me ready to attack
Taking all my will-power to hold it back.
There is no cure for this disease,
Nobody can take away what my eyes did see,
The torture and pain will always be there,
Hidden from a society who tends not to care.
Learning to oppress my PTSD
Will enable me to fit neatly into society,
Not getting to close to the people close by,
Keeping them at distance to avoid the pry.
My eyes are brown and full of woe,
Look deep into them: you will be shocked what they show...

The mantras helped me adjust to a completely different way of life, where I had to make my own destiny and my mind wasn't being controlled on which pathway to follow. The military taught me and showed me some amazing things; however, like all good friends there are times when they should have been there and weren't changing the perception of friendship to control.

Whilst my outside persona always signalled happiness, my inside was torn in two with thoughts and feelings of the past that I had no control or understanding of. Still resistant to help, I used my friend in my head, the poet, to help me: instead of dwelling on terrible thoughts and feelings, I wrote them down, thus ensuring they could be filed away and forgotten – hopefully.

Shouting in a Box

The room is crowded, and you feel the only one there,
The noise is loud but the silence in your head you can't bear.
When people see you but you don't exist,
You want to scream but quietly resist.
People can't see the darkness inside,
They're too wrapped up in their own busy lives.
When thoughts overtake reality itself,
Be aware to protect your mental health.
Look after this, it will look after you,
Getting help while you can will pull you through.
When you see life on the other side,
You will take depression in your stride.
There are people to help take the pain away,
Friends are around – you just have to say.
Getting through troubles is easy as a team,
Life isn't really as bad as it does seem.

Writing how to get some help and things are not so bad was my "masking process" to try and help others rather than look at my demons themselves and get the help I needed at this time. As the winter months started, the people I saw got fewer, giving my mind the ability to run off in all tangents. Looking back at this point, I realise this is the point I should have asked for help. My decision to weather the storm took me down a very dark path, contemplating my life and its meaning and looking for lighter days.

Dark versus Light

A mundane life trapped in a cage ,
Nothing to excite, just anger and rage,
A mental state of a stormy time,
With a mountain of hope unable to climb.
The darker days are here again,
The destruction of life and depletion of men,
A mental state bought on by a curse,
A situation which is getting worse.
A crime of the mind an invisible fight,
When the daylight is dark no matter how bright,
A moment in time, a fleeting back thought
Of a happy memory in the past a dream was caught.
Holding onto this light to fight to survive,
The darkest moments the mind contrives,
Keeping the light close to your heart,
Beams of light trigger and start.
Soon the day is a brighter place,
And the grey matt finish is removed from your face.
Every morning the conflict begins:
Dark versus light, a fight against sin.

My life followed a path of the struggle of darkness for a long time. Being able to see it as a struggle against two factors enabled me to understand the depths and the highs of the war in my mind.

Darkness into light

When darkness smothers light
And the day turns into night,
The shadows are no longer there.
Doubt takes over,
The room gets colder
And the feelings are of grief and despair.
There is a fear of the unknown,
Imagination of horrors are shown
And the support is no longer there.
As the darkness fades
And happiness parades,
The light returns to the world.
The shadows are back
But fear they do lack
As the power of light unfolds.

Constantly experiencing this battle, when I received dark thoughts I would attack them with lighter, happier thoughts, using the power of my poet to fight alongside next to me. Strangely, it worked to start off with. However, as the moments got darker even light couldn't break through the density of the fog.

Am I ILL?

I'm angry, I'm sad,
I'm calm, I'm mad,
I'm indecisive, I know what I need,
All of these things and nothing more,
I'm scared to even open my front door.
My brain says one thing, my body says no,
I never know which way to go.
I ask for help, guidance and direction,
The other side follows my healthy reflection.
I'm nervous, I'm scared: am I ill?
Can someone prescribe a sanity pill?
I need help, understanding, love and care
And a group of people with which to share,
Share my story, my dark strange life,
And why I cut myself with a blunt serrated knife.
I'm not mad, I'm unsure with nowhere to belong,
I will fight my war and progress remain strong.
Soon I will look back on my mystery,
Laugh and joke about my jaded history,
Remembering, though, it will always be there,
My life in the shadows.
Don't look close or stare.

Convinced now that I had an illness and that I wasn't going mad, I wondered if there was a pill that could sort it all out. Still using my poet to fight the demons as I moved through the dark times, some days of which I didn't even know who I was, pausing to try and recognise the person in the pictures and the mirror.

The Poet Is My Friend

Depression, anxiety, fatigue and pain,
Bad decisions are made and thoughts of disdain:
When will I understand my true mental state?
As thousands of workers attack and create,
They create a world where no man can live,
With thoughts and dreams I can't deal with,
A parallel world with feelings amiss,
When there is no blue sky, just a dark abyss.
Fighting my war with a dark, tainted brain,
The things it remembers drive me insane.
My poet will help me fight the dark days,
Cleansing the mind with healthier ways.
A hard thing to crack, being mentally aware;
Lots will fail and try not to dare.
Many can help in this fight for the light,
There is no correct way of turning black to white.

Deciding now to include the reality of my poet as my medication and supporting arm, the power of my words grew stronger. Feelings were now being displaced onto paper like an overflow of mind games and weapons up for display. I was also very aware now that I could be progressing towards a split personality. However, with nobody else to talk to I realised that this may not be a bad thing, as it would at least help me with the loneliness and its constant attacks on my well-being and altering mental states.

Caged in a Zoo

Behind the bars or in a cage,
Nobody will understand my rage.
In a tank or in a pool
Laughed at pointed at and treated like a fool.
On a lead or in a shackle,
Smiled at, laughed at and even a heckle.
But left to roam, they stretch their legs,
Sniffing the air temptation does beg,
The grass is greener on the other side,
Or is it?
Do the bars, shackles and tanks protection provide?
Hidden from life itself,
The ever-present dangers of mental health,
Safety to be cared for in a public place,
Protected and sterilised in a safe space.
I need this kind of safety too:
Is it a part of my life to live in a zoo?

As I explored the causes of my re-occurring dark thoughts, my poet always seemed to lead me onto the path of freedom. Mentioning that I was caged and should be free was a very strange concept for me, as I have been in the military for such a long time at a young age and now was stuck in a life with a time frame and another cage. I would soon realise that the myriad of problems I encountered would have to be addressed by myself, and although my poet was doing a fantastic job, all he was doing was identifying the problems and causes.

Find My Way

On a mind-blowing day,
How do I find my way?
When the weather is bad,
How do I find my way?
When unmotivated and sad,
How do I find my way?
When there seems no reason to carry on,
How do I find my way?
When I feel all hope has gone,
How do I find my way?
I look round, and what have I got?
That is how I find my way:
I look at what others have not.
That is how I find my way:
I immerse myself in the love of my friends.
That's how I find my way:
I look on whom does depend.
That's how I find my way:
I thank myself I'm lucky to be alive.
That's how I find my way
I look at others and how they've cried
That's how I find my way:
Be grateful for what is yours and what you do
And you will always find your way.
Stay truthful on the path of life,
And forever you will find your way.

---

*I realised that as the days changed and the night drew in,
so did my dark cloud. Boredom would also place me in posi-
tions where I would question, "What's the point?" But with
everything I would always have an answer from the poet, and
more often than not that would set me up for the day. There
were days when my questions were deeper, more about my
sanity than depression.*

Brain Control Insane

I need you close,
You hide my morose.
I'm comfortable when you're near.
What are you?
What do you do?
I cannot understand
The power you command.
You are there when I least expect
And challenge me with what I will do next.
You fill me full of happiness
And put me under complexed duress.
How I need you by my side,
My subconscious life guide:
A strange name
To call my brain,
The working, hidden, other me
That the world cannot actually see.
More complex than the cleverest computer,
This being already knows your future.

Dropping deeper into the complexity of who was actually running the show, me or the poet, I would write one myself. They were always a little bit obscure and had some interference from the other me but still paved the way through life – my life – my secret life. Things hadn't changed that much since my military days. Years ago I would hide my sexuality for fear of getting imprisoned and losing everything; now I'm hiding the fact I have a relationship with myself and in my opinion it's two of us – not one!

Inside the Human Form

Disturbed not perturbed,
Not deranged or absurd,
Simple not complexed,
Focussed not perplexed,
Different yet magnificent,
Easy-going, no aggression pent:
The person inside is what we really hide,
Seeing what's real,
Handling how that makes you feel.
All makes us special in our own way,
Complete understanding yet utter dismay
Of how people can behave,
With thoughts that hurt and are depraved.
The inside person we should not ignore
Behind good, evil can be at the core;
On the opposite side,
Good can hide
Behind anger and repression,
The smoke of depression and fear.
Good can be behind that rolling tear.
Judging what you see is a difficult matter,
For the mind's illusion reality can shatter.

The fact that I was able to be two people and nobody actually knew meant that the problems I had could be turned off when I swapped over to the other. That went for both people, as the poet would have perplexed problems too. But obviously the poet wasn't real – or was he? And the real me was the made-up one – or was it? Having this feeling made me reach the crossroads we all reach when a decision needs to be made about what path to take.

Scared to Exist

As my heart beats,
I feel that time does deplete
And I have no purpose anymore.
The world still turns
And my mind yearns
To discover what my life is for.
Do I need to express
My lack of interest
About the dealings of the world today.
Should I shout out loud
Or remain quiet and proud,
Hiding the fact I am this way?
Would people care
If I was no longer there
And my opinion wouldn't matter anymore?
I feel unable to say
With some dismay
And hide behind a lonely closed door.
One day I will shout
And let it all out,
Amid my fears of normal society.
Until that day
This is how I will stay
Until confidence builds up inside of me.

Both the inner poet and I had our doubts about reality. However, one thing that was decided is that the world wasn't ready for a public performance. Therefore we would stay hidden, sharing the day between us. Both were scared to exist as neither really wanted to face reality.

Change of Life

I don't want this life anymore,
Its time to hang up my coat and head for the door.
I'm relied on constantly,
Nobody thinks about the inside me.
I don't want this life anymore
I don't want to go to work today,
I am in bed, warm and I want to stay.
The treadmill of life
Cuts deep like a knife
And I think it's time I had my say.
I don't want to listen to the voice,
Stop talking, I feel I have no choice.
If you have nothing interesting to say,
Go quietly about your day,
So I can hear other things bar your voice.
I'm happier on my own,
I rarely feel exposed or alone.
So what I'm trying to say
Is stay out of my way,
In my rude and angry tone.
My life's really not that bad
I look at what I've got and had.
Some people have nowt,
They are angry and shout,
So I should look at my life and be glad.

Strangely, as the year moved on the poet and I were often harmonious, however sometimes at conflict as to which one of us was the real person. The poet would always still motivate me when times were sad and dark and I would always give myself a kick when I was drowning in a word ocean, spurting poetry left right and centre and completing little else. One thing was for sure, though: as a team we were brilliant, separate not so good, so decisions would have to be made in the future to preserve both our sanities.

Tough Life

Never give up when things get tough,
They will get better, they are only rough.
Fight on through to the other side,
Get your mind set and do not hide,
For life itself can be cruel
And it will take you for a fool
If you don't get on and take control,
Ensuring that happiness is your goal.
Learning through mistakes is a hard game,
Trying again will never bring shame.
Helping someone in their hour of need
Will allow you both not to concede,
For when things are bad get tough and ask
"How will I complete this task?"
To succeed you do not need to be successful,
Realising your boundaries shouldn't be stressful.
Realise potential, complete your goals,
Avoid the drop down a long deep hole.
When you're happy, look back and laugh
And say to yourself, "Long may it last!"

Darkness seems to be far from my thoughts now. Poet and I are on track to succeed, with motivating poems from him and a set of new challenges for me. All seemed to be going well, but we had forgotten about the PTSD.

Mantra of a Modern Man

See inside the beauty,
Feel inside the joy,
Grapple with intelligence,
Love is but a joy.
Wrestle with your anger,
Taste the real pain,
Argue you with righteousness,
Question you're insane.
Stand fast in front of abstinence,
Hold on to the cause,
Study intellectuality,
Avoid starting new wars.
Never doubt yourself
Wherever you may be,
Stand mighty, tall and proud
So all the universe can see.
Never hold back on feelings,
Always do what you can:
Before you is the mantra
Of a thoroughly modern man.

Poems and odes of self-motivation were now fast becoming the wind in my wings; the poet and I seemed to work together with these. My days improved and life had more purpose. Dark clouds were dissipating and the sun came out, something that I haven't seen in a while.

I continued on my rebuilding exercise, with constant reminders from the poet about how I should live my life. Was I losing a grip on myself and being steered in a different direction? Probably. However, this direction seemed an awful lot brighter than my past and so, while all was going well, I kept at it.

Trust in Animosity

Find trust in animosity,
Forget all the hurt you see.
Try and treat life carefully
And happy you will be.
Ignore any recompense,
Try not to make any sense
Of fate and its capability,
And happy you will be.
Find the love inside of you,
Staying calm and remaining true.
Think of others in all you do,
And happy you will be.
Enjoy every moment within your life,
Stay away from trouble and strife,
Taking care of body and mind,
And happy you will be.
When you get upset a bit,
Try not to get fed up of it.
Look forward to every day,
And happy you will stay.

I was very conscious now that my life was being led by a poet, also a poet that did not actually exist! Days now seemed to turn into lessons from my alter ego. Was I happy with this? For the time being, yes, as it was definitely the easier option than facing the reality of my life, its past and the dark places that went along with it. I often got angry and questioned why I pushed myself so much to succeed, and even questioned what success actually is/was.

What Is Success?

What is success?
Is it how you look and how you dress?
What is success?
Is it how you act, who you impress?
Am I a success?
Do people say thanks under duress?
Is there a need to achieve?
There is an expectation, I perceive:
From a young age we are encouraged,
But forcefulness can often discourage.
Success and achievement can make you smile;
Stop or pause take a breath for a while.
Success can be the first step to winning life's lottery,
Completing a task to break the monotony.
So I conclude if you are living you are already a success,
For life is so hard and so full of stress.
Getting to the end of every day,
You should pat yourself on the back and say,
"I achieved, am happy and a success,"
And wait for the next day you can impress –
Success!!

After weeks of joyful, motivating poems which started to turn into lessons and lectures about the man I should be, I started to think... Never a good idea, as it invokes memories of past dark days and opens the book to other thoughts and mind twists. However, I continued to think about my journey and what stage I was at. Thoughts of the past churned my stomach and made me scared about my future. Thinking is definitely a decision I should think about in the future...

Thinking...

I have a funny feeling in my stomach pit,
It's strange and confusing and I'm scared of it.
The feelings make me worried and full of anxiety,
It's a really funny feeling like a whirlpool inside of me.
I'm usually confident, outward and brash,
Not bothered even if I happen to crash,
But this time I'm anxious, jittery and jumpy,
And my mood swings range from happy to grumpy.
Why is this so different to my normal ways?
I've faced bigger problems on much worse days.
But still the feeling remains,
It makes me tired as my confidence drains.
How will I fight the pitted snake
Standing tall and to mobilise without looking fake?
Being myself, taking control of my actions,
Looking above all the distracting factions,
For nerves are only a state of mind,
People see them and can be unkind.
So the best way of dealing with this mental state
Is trust yourself and don't be fake.

The thoughts I was having were starting to change my pathway of light into darker days again, a road I definitely didn't want to head down. Thoughts were running deep now and I realised that the poet had been with me for a long time, helping me through a lot of mental health disasters which all started with the battle with my sexuality and ability to understand it myself, in a world that wasn't ready to understand it with me.

Clairvoyant Sexual Preference

I read my tea leaves the other day:
A rainbow was discovered, so I'm obviously gay.
I wish it was that easy to decide,
Fighting masculinity and femininity inside.
To select one was my generation's choice,
Whether to shout aloud or have a quiet voice.
In the military it was still oppressed,
Leaving people suicidal and depressed.
To be told you cannot be who you want to be inside
Is like taking away a twin which you had to hide,
A twin who was happy and only you could see
Who was joyful, funny and able to be free.
Releasing the twin didn't change much,
The stigma was there and cruel to the touch.
So me and the twin of opposite feelings
Will dip our toe and have a few dealings,
Always keeping my identity well hidden
In a country when being yourself is forbidden.

Sexuality caused the most challenging time of my life. Having to go through this stage and to hide it broke and split me in two. This was the birth of the poet, and unfortunately the birth of the poet signified a death of part of my identity. I'm thankful for the career the RAF gave me, but I will never forgive them for how much of my life and identity they took away. People received compensation for losing their jobs; however, there could be no type of compensation that would replace the damage to my mental state and oppression of the real me. Thankfully, the poet was there when the RAF was not!

The Curse

The curse is not knowing who will accept,
Who will comply and who will reject,
Who will get angry, judgemental and mad,
Who will be upset, melancholy and sad,
Who will be welcoming, pleased and coy,
Who will be accepting, hard to annoy.
Knowing the above will help you explore
Your sexuality and what's worth fighting for,
A secret best kept but able to tell,
Certainly a subject to ponder and dwell.
Making a decision need not happen fast,
Try all circumstances, matters not if they last,
Remembering always to be happy and true,
Being yourself in all you do.
Hiding the worry will break the man:
He will not fulfil all he can.
Be loud and proud whatever you are,
Keep it truthful and you will go far.

Taking decisions without guidance always sets you up for a fall: somebody will always get hurt, annoyed, angry or frustrated. Talking to yourself and the decisions you made from your inner conversation shape your whole life. In circumstances like this, I was pleased to have the poet with me – but remembering the past and its struggles pulls back the darkness in my history once more...

Changing Light

It's dark now,
I can feel the sweat dripping from my brow.
I feel it near me,
The scariest thing my eyes could see,
The thing that dries my mouth right out,
The beast that scared me so much I shout,
The thing with teeth bigger than me,
The demon that lurks only I can see,
The thing with piercing eyes of red,
Watching and waiting, careful where I tread,
Lurking in the dark shadows,
Waiting in places where only I go.
I should surrender to its mighty fear,
Not allowing it close, feeling its heat, it's near.
One day it will pounce, all will be revealed,
Ugliness and pain it will always yield.
I know this creature is not real,
As it takes control of me and how I feel.

Changing PTSD into a physical creature enables me to identify it as an actual being that I am able to fight against or relate to. Seeing a physical being gives me the ability to believe the problem is real. As I descended further into darkness yet again for this fight, I would need my strength and the strength of the poet to pull me through – knowing that I was not only dealing with my PTSD from the military but was also dealing with my sexuality demon and confidence, areas against which I had been able to win easily in the past and was now finding it harder than ever in the future to understand the issues that they once caused.

Approaching another crossroads within my life, I was now faced with a myriad of emotional paths, all of which had to be followed to be rectified and to restore my sanity to my perception of normal (if that exists).

Emotional Crossroads

Paths that take me in different ways,
Some with mistakes and the end of days,
Some with fun happiness and joy,
Some that take me back to that boy,
That boy that didn't know which way to turn,
With carnal desires and a body that yearned.
Some paths that stop just after they begin,
Paths that no matter what you will win,
But which to take and which way to go,
To allow a good path and my mind to grow?
Down the path of darkness, it seems,
Searching for light and all that gleams,
Heading for happiness and a stable way,
Trusting reality and the truth of a day.
Decisions that face my world every day,
Down the cul de sac of decisions, destination GAY.

Preparing for my journey ahead, leaving my pathways unde-cided, I relied upon my inner poet to guide me using subcon-scious thoughts and dreams in my quest, I wasn't insane or turning that way, I was deciding how to get through my life without asking for mental guidance. Now was the time the voices in my head would turn either against or for me, shaping my future and making my decisions.

My Mate Me

I had such a deep sleep I dreamt I couldn't wake,
Realised it was a wish I just couldn't take.
My mind works in such funny ways,
Changing the course of my structured days.
The hidden voice within my head
Talks me through my decisions in bed,
Putting them right for the perfect path
Or igniting the fire to feed the wrath.
I talk to myself but nobody hears,
I listen to myself but rarely adhere,
I rebel against my own decision,
Question my style, thoughts and precision,
Sometimes knowing it's the argument I will win,
Starting a story I didn't want to begin.
I'm happy that I is now a we,
We make decisions on how it will be.
I'm often right but we usually are,
With a team like that we are over the bar.
Knowing that I am ready to fight what comes next,
With a mind that is clear, not challenged and perplexed.

Now totally aware that this was the beginning of a full-on mental health war and the outcome of this would have a lasting affect on my future, I summoned as much courage from within as I could and teamed with the poet to face what the future would throw at us. Aware that I was now entering what many would call a fantasy state, I was tickled to picture myself in armour with a poet at my side fighting dragons and demons, a fictional state that wasn't actually far from the truth.

Inner Cause- the Fight Begins

Heartache in the wake of a tear,
As bad news rises so does the fear,
Damaging reality on how we live,
Enabling selfishness and the point to forgive.
Surviving the journey all on your own,
The seed has been planted and now it has grown,
The start of the future, its new life and meaning,
Putting into fruition plans you've been dreaming.
The force of fate and how it controls
Destiny and life and your hidden trolls,
Using the time relieves the pressure,
The stress of anxiety does not get lesser.
What goes on in the human mind
When it's pushed in a corner and life is unkind,
The survival instinct reveals inside
The body is strong, mental issues we hide.
It's all just a century-long fight,
Make your life different, hold onto the light.
Through the darkness the light does shine,
Colour and happiness will fall in line.
When all is good in this world of yours,
You've discovered your reason and true inner cause.

The fight continued in my mind about what was expected of me and what I actually was. Aware that I probably didn't know myself, what I actually was, the fight became a self-exploration journey, opening my mind to new feelings and opportunities whilst reminding me of the dark past and how it wants to consume me. Motivation being my strongest weapon, we were now ready to fight and fight hard against the darkness.

Motivational Madness

Don't dream it, be it.
Don't look at it, see it.
Strive for perfection,
Laugh at the reflection.
Don't dream it, be it.
Don't promise it, do it.
Don't question it, get through it.
Make new memories,
Be your own celebrity.
Don't promise it, do it.
Don't be scared of it,
Conquer it.
Work hard and achieve,
Don't worry, just believe,
But never be scared of it.
Don't hide it, be proud,
Don't hide your life behind a shroud,
For only you know
How much you can grow.
Don't hide it, just be proud,
Be yourself when you can,
It won't make you a lesser man.
The persona comes from inside,
And only cowards will hide.
Be yourself if you can.

Whilst fighting against the dark mental health issues you face on a daily basis, it is important to keep and stay on the path of the morals which are deep-set within you. These are defined from birth and shape people as people; they are your individualisation against your fight with mental health. The poet fights with words, we fight with morals.

Fighting with Words

They're fighting in the suburbs ,
Not with weapons just with words.
They're shouting without noise,
The silenced protestors the world annoys.
They're writing paragraphs of lies,
They call it news, it's a public disguise.
Who are they?
And why do they have an impact on my day?
They are you,
And everything you do not do.
You fight with words
And give up as though unheard.
You shout, but nobody hears,
So shout louder until they adhere.
You write lies,
Nobody takes notice or does compromise.
Find your voice,
Make your choice.
Get noticed,
Which will show progress.
Don't be blended a shade of grey,
Letting your life slip away.
Be the person you know you are,
Because you are in demand, your skill will take you far.

Whilst falling deeper into my darker places I was "virtually kicked" by my poet to remind me of the things inside of me that make me great and separate me from the crowd - the maddening crowd. Throughout my fight against my dark mental state, it triggered emotional changes within in me, which then in turn affected the people around me. My secret fight against my mental state was in danger of spilling out into the open; once in the open, it would be judged and I would again lose identity.

The Weather Does Change

The sky turned black.
So did my mind.
I dispelled happiness,
Replaced with unkind.
Compassion was exchanged,
Only jealousy remained.

The day the sky turned black
And the rain came down,
Smile was replaced with a frown.
Heartache grew,
Sadness came through,
The day the rain came down.
When the snow blew through,
It ignited the happiness I once knew.
Through frost-bit ears
And crystal tears
The day the snow blew through,
The day the sun beamed on.
My darkness had gone,
The warmth touched my face.
Body filled with grace,
The day the sun beamed on.
When the weather does change,
Emotions are stirred and rearranged.
Changes occur,
Memories are a blur,
When the weather does change.

Realising that my inner mental state would change as often as the weather, I longed for brighter days. In the dead of winter, when days are grey, often bringing a darkened cloak onto life itself, you can feel that there is no end to the prolonged darkness. However, once the realisation occurs that mental states are like seasons, a gleam of light hits, whether its from the brightness of snow or that sighting of a beam of light linked to spring or a storm-free, brighter day which sits on the horizon awaiting a chance to bloom. The difference between realisation and what is happening at this moment can seem more of a fable than fact. As this war continues, the poet and I encounter many a parallel and many a tool to use in the future in our fight against the dark...

There's No Way Out

There is no way out.
I'm stuck in a box
Surrounded by chains and covered in locks.
Nobody knows the pain I've got.
I want my life to end.
I have voices in my head
Filling my stomach full of dread,
Shouting at me and wanting me dead.
I want my life to end.
It's a fever that comes over me,
Making me run hide and flee.
It's not how I want my life to be.
I want my life to end.
There is nobody that would understand,
Nobody around to hold my hand.
All I need in life is a friend.
I want my life to end.
Having a person to talk to,
Helping me and guiding me through,
Reminding me I'm not one of the few,
Whose life isn't ready to end.

Questioning everything like normal, I would sometimes debate my sanity, as it wasn't natural to hear voices- or was it? Having nobody to actually talk to about this, and concerned that if I did talk to somebody I would be given help in a nice hotel with white padded walls, I often had a little debate with my self as to why I should live. I found when this happened, I was able to ensure that I stayed alive, as either I or the poet, or both as one, would convince myself that life was worth living and even though I don't know what it actually is, I do have a purpose. Although on this roller coaster of depression or maybe just life, I had good days – oh, and some bad days and days where I couldn't actually understand anything at all. I called it my "dreams to nightmare" phase!

Dreams to Nightmares

One day you're happy, one day you're sad,
Some days are quiet, others are mad.
Life seems to run on extremes,
Turning once-feared nightmares into lovely dreams.
Surviving life can be tough,
Nothing is smooth, all is rough.
Money is scarce and living is hard,
Life deals you a losing card.
Life runs on extremes,
Turning nightmares into dreams.
There is always a turning point in this world,
When bad luck depletes, good luck enfolds.
Its not the path all of us do take,
Some are distracted and make mistakes.
Whichever way you choose to turn,
Always remember to take heed and learn.
Life runs on extremes,
Some have nightmares, some have dreams.
Whichever direction that you chose,
Remember you can never lose,
For life and love are a winning game,
You're in control and you're to blame.
If the direction is not the right one,
Go back to the path from where it begun.
Life runs fine, you make it extreme:
Try turning nightmares into good dreams.

The further into depression this journey takes me, I find sign-posts along the way to help me back, soon realising if my life is as truly unhappy as I say it is, I am the only one to be able to change it for the better. So it's up to me with the help of the poet to deplete the negativity. It was time to bring myself out of this mundane cloak of depression with my friend the poet helping me all the way. Strange that I now am two people, and comforting in a way, as it's just you and me!!

Just You and Me

It's easy to run from the pain inside,
To not face the music to run and hide,
To forget all the trouble caused and begun,
Turning your back and pretending you won.
There are no winners in this world of ours,
No hidden escapes or super powers.
We have only our conscience to rely upon.
Tackling these problems won't take long.
Releasing all anxiety and pain,
Putting away hate and disdain,
Seeing a clear picture of what life should be,
Continuing our journey, just you and me.

Skipping off Wizard of Oz style down the Yellow Brick Road of life, the poet and I are on our way up and continue our fight against the black dog SADS...

Black Dog SADS...

As winter unfolds, my black dog arrives,
The dark cloud that covers my lonely life,
The heavy burden that won't go away,
The lonely blanket covering every day.
The feelings and thoughts running through my head
Put me on the long path of solitude instead.
I feel that there is no end in sight,
Now my consciousness has turned off the tunnel light.
It takes all my energy to face the day,
The option is bed and self-pity to lay.
I immerse myself in things that are good
To show me the way through the darkened woods.
Eat well, socialise, talk away the pain,
There are more than you feeling exactly the same.
Share the low points, enhance the high,
Take a shoulder, have a good cry.
Nobody understands what your mind puts you through,
The unfortunate thoughts you are subjected to.
Make that call, it helps to share,
Make that friend completely aware
That it's always winter, you suffer a lot,
Sharing will help, the pain will blot.
Carry on with the daily routine,
Fighting the illness which is suffered and rarely seen.

Understanding that depression and anxiety constitute an illness is the first step to getting better. There are many routes to get well, and your mind will tell you which way to go. Poetry is my way forward as it gives me reasoning as to why my feelings are behaving so strangely.

Understanding why these things are happening to me, I decided to build on my life, now encompassing the poet in all I do, as between us we are a formidable team...

Build on Life

I delved deep into my mind,
Not too sure what I would find.
There is so much I've been through
That only I ever knew.
I go past all the weird stuff
Like a tortoise wearing a muff!
I enter the different zones
To all the places I've called home:
The Middle East with its conflict,
The difference in culture, places I don't fit,
To the war-torn worlds in which I served,
To the 100 bullets my body has swerved,
To the happy places,
The secret spaces,
The places I go to think,
Back to the areas of my life once ruled by drink,
The different pathways I would take,
The million mistakes I would make,
The happy times, the sad times,
My innocent world, my heinous crimes.
I decide not to go back but to forward-think,
Now the page is empty and I have the ink.
More mistakes I'm sure will be made,
But new bricks will be built and new foundations laid.

Forward-thinking and looking at the amazing things I could do with my future life enables me to look at an empty page and fill it with happiness and hope. I the brain is indeed a computer: this is a mental health reboot.

Mental Reboot

Diving inside the mind,
Working through emotions hurtful and unkind,
The complexity of thoughts,
Of aspirations and misery caught,
Or anger, contempt, and rage,
Of plans and considerations already made,
Anticipation of future events,
Of happier times and days well spent,
The maze of madness deep inside.
A smiling face this mask does hide,
The dark cloud effecting the psyche,
Wired up wrong, malfunction likely.
Chemicals adjust the negative ways,
Bringing drug-induced happier days,
But the wiring can deteriorate
And problems with health and mind create,
Causing the well-feared blue screen of doom.
The internal hard drive now has no room
Without the option to reboot
Or the ability to troubleshoot.
So that's it, switch off restart,
The rewire will complete the start.
But beware, the malfunction can lie dormant in wait:
Seek help or the failed repair will seal your fate.

Just with everything in life, it seems that if you stop, turn it off and restart it again the problem goes away temporarily. Some people live their lives sticking to this routine, but to get to the bottom of the problem and fix the problem before reboot will ensure the program runs continuously without problems developing in the future! Especially recurring past problems. Having spent the majority of my adult life so far fighting one demon or another, I have to ask myself: how long do we have? How long do I have? How long do you have?

How Long?...

Time travels so fast,
You hang onto every minute
To make the day last.
You clutch every hour
To stop it fading away,
For when they add up, gone is the day.
You cherish every week
As they fly by,
As soon as one starts another one is nigh.
They fade to months
As the calendar moves on.
Blink and you will miss it,
That's a year gone.
Soon a decade has come and passed.
Childhood has vanished,
How long did it last?
Soon you look back on days gone by,
They are slowing down now,
No matter how hard you try.
As you hold onto the minutes
In times that have gone,
Make every one count,
As we don't know how long.

It's one thing that propels my future forward after all that I've been through. Everybody says, "Live for tomorrow, not today." I think they are wrong: live for today and each minute, because as every one passes you won't get it back. Certainly, live your best life in every minute of every day. As I pass through this bout of depression with the help of my poet, who as always is by my side, taking my own advice I look back as to what could be the cause, the root of the problem, and I believe it to be my identity as a man. Am I a man? Does it matter if I'm not? And what makes a man?

What Makes a Man?

What makes a man?
Is it physical?
Not at all, appearance does not make a man.
Is a man strong and brave?
He can be, but compassion he must not deprave.
Is a man selfish and stubborn?
Some are, yes, but most are considerate often.
Is a man always the boss?
If he is, it's only his loss.
Does a man have to be physically complete?
Not at all, it's the inside we seek.
So a man can be anyone at all,
It's only a label which wasn't your call.
So who are we if we are not defined?
There is no written law if you're not that way inclined.
So what makes a man?
The person inside;
The warm glow of love and protection he hides;
The will to succeed and admit defeat;
The ability to stand on your own two feet.
No different to a woman this day and age,
Both are people who bring home a wage.
So what makes a man is the question I ask?
Anybody strong enough to complete all life's tasks.

So finally I conquer my demons and the root of it all was my sexuality and my ability to be a man. It took so many problems in so many scenarios to actually understand that being a man is facing and conquering my fears, whoever and whatever they are, and achieving true happiness in myself. Life will always throw me curve-balls and I will continue on the journey picking pathways which are wrong and right, but remembering that as long as I am happy, I'm on the right path.

So for the first time in a long time I'm content with my life.

Content with Your Life

If you are happy and you know it,
Don't be afraid to show it.
If you have a talent, grow it,
And be content with your life.
If you have a point to prove,
Say it, don't be shrewd,
Be eloquent, not crude,
And be content with your life.
Life for you, not others,
Treat all friends like brothers,
Be respectful to your lovers,
And be content with your life.
If you feel you're not,
You want what someone else has got,
Be a statement, not a blot,
And be content with your life.
If you feel like it's out of reach,
Look at others to learn, not to teach.
Take advice, use it like a leech
And be content with your life.
On your deathbed closing words,
This is what should be heard:
"I was happy, I was sad,
But I'm content with my life."

Another episode of my life comes to an end, and having fought my depression, anxiety and fears with my friend the poet, we continue to work together and find ourselves at another cross-roads. Which path will I take this time?

To be continued ...